History of Philosophy II

UNI SLOVAKIA series
Volume 12

History of Philosophy II
Plato and Aristotle

Michal Zvarík

Bibliographic Information published by the Deutsche Nationalbibliothek

The Deutsche Nationalbibliothek lists this publication in the Deutsche Nationalbibliografie; detailed bibliographic data is available in the internet at http://dnb.d-nb.de

The publication of this book is part of the project Support for Improving the Quality of Trnava University (ITMS code 26110230092) — preparation of a Liberal Arts study program, which was supported by the European Union via its European Social Fund and by the Slovak Ministry of Education within the Operating Program Education. The text was prepared at the Department of Philosophy, Faculty of Philosophy, Trnava University in Trnava.

Design and Layout: © Jana Sapáková, Layout JS.
Printing: VEDA, Publishing House of the Slovak Academy of Sciences

ISSN 2366-2697
ISBN 978-3-631-67463-5
E-ISBN 978-3-653-06649-4
DOI 10.3726/978-3-653-06649-4

© Peter Lang GmbH
Internationaler Verlag der Wissenschaften
Frankfurt am Main 2016

All rights reserved.

Peter Lang Edition is an Imprint of Peter Lang GmbH.
Peter Lang – Frankfurt am Main · Bern · Bruxelles · New York · Oxford · Warszawa · Wien

All parts of this publication are protected by copyright. Any utilisation outside the strict limits of the copyright law, without the permission of the publisher, is forbidden and liable to prosecution. This applies in particular to reproductions, translations, microfilming, and storage and processing in electronic retrieval systems.

This publication has been peer reviewed.

www.peterlang.com

Contents

Introduction	7
Plato	11
1. Life	13
2. Work	17
3. Concept of the Idea	25
4. Anamnésis and Knowledge	29
5. Plato's Analogies	37
6. Soul and City	59
Aristotle	69
1. Life	71
2. Work	73
3. *Organon* and the Theory of Cognition	77
4. Metaphysics and the Structure of the *Cosmos*	85
5. Ethics	95
List of Abbreviations	106
Bibliography	107

Introduction

In the 5th century BC, through the activities of the sophists, the classical period of Greek philosophy begins, especially the period which is famous thanks to the names of the three renowned men: Socrates, Plato, and Aristotle. If it is true that Socrates and the sophists focused their attention mainly on the human being at the expense of natural investigations, Plato and Aristotle in their plans achieved a new unity and its deepening in the nascent metaphysics. Sophists strongly questioned the possibility of knowledge and how it is distinguished from opinion, their development of Aporia stated that nothing can be said with certainty, and that the core of a happy life lies rather in the ability to convince than to have expertise, respectively. The highest state of knowledge and proficiency is the ability to convince. In this way they stated the serious issues with which Plato and Aristotle dealt. The answer was an effort to develop a complex view, resulting in a vision of the *cosmos* as a hierarchical regulation of causes. In it a man does not act as the measure of all things, on the contrary, he is understood as something inherently "between" and is an imperfect being between God and animals and his life is the struggle between the possibilities of low physical life, the life of cattle, as Aristotle says and the high theoretical life in which he most fully develops his possibilities and can then be likened to the divine.

One of Plato's key answers to the sophists is a concept of the idea, as an eternal and perfect being, according to which it is not created, only perceived by the senses and is an imperfect picture of things, but in ethical behaviour it should serve as a standard by which we should manage and arrange our lives. Thus, the idea is not only a distant metaphysical concept; it touches practical life and not only the life of individuals but also the common, shared, and political life of the city (*polis*). In contrast, Aristotle develops logic as an instrument of control of our thoughts that reveals misleading arguments, it also points out that we can live our life best, if we devote ourselves to theoretical research. In ethics he adjusts Protagoras's *homo mensura*, the thesis that the measure of all things is a capable man who knows how to act properly and wants to act in that way.

These are only some of the initiatives by which Plato and Aristotle unmistakably influenced European and global spiritual history. Their importance extends far beyond their time and their works represented a major voice practically in all subsequent periods. They influenced not only the form of ancient philosophy, but practically since the turn of the millennium they served as the philosophical basis for scientific research, the rationale of mystical experiences or prophetic religions. A trend that lasted until the High Middle Ages. They are still not forgotten; they are a source of inspiration for phenomenology or hermeneutics. It is worth mentioning the growing interest in ethical, political, and social reflections, where the feelings and understanding of humans as imperfect beings often serves as a sober barrier against the emptiness of current ideologies. Thus, there are a lot of reasons why we should deal with Plato and Aristotle. It would be a mistake to treat them as historical figures that have nothing to tell us. They allow us to look at the present through the prism of their work, taking a critical distance towards it and so providing interesting new insights. There is no textbook which could replace an in depth study of the primary texts. Not even this book aspires to it. It is rather a result of the effort to assist those who are interested in this area to have an initial orientation.

Plato

1. Life

Plato was born in Athens in 427 BC. The key sources of information about his life are mainly the *Lives of Eminent Philosophers* by Diogenes Laertius and the seventh of Plato's Letters. He came from an aristocratic family, from his father Ariston he traced his origin from the mythical king Codrus and further to Poseidon. Similarly aristocratic is the family of his mother Perictione whose origins were similar to his father's, so it starts at Poseidon and continues through the famous statesman Solon. Plato's relatives are often characters in his dialogues. Two of his dialogues are named after Critias, the cousin of his mother and her brother Charmides, and in The Republic we can meet Plato's brothers Glauconand and Adeimantus. Diogenes incidentally states that Plato was born on the same day of the year as the god Apollo and was even conceived by him (DL III, 2). These reports show that Plato's person was later attributed legendary and divine features.

In his youth, Plato acquired a good education, allegedly took part in the Olympics, and wanted to dedicate his life to writing tragedies. Ultimately he was discouraged from writing when he met Socrates and he became his student at the age of 20. Plato's life was deeply marked by contemporary political turbulence. We learn about his attitude toward it especially from the *Seventh Letter*. Athenian democracy, which flourished mostly after the Persian wars and during the reign of Pericles, which was spent in endless battles of Sparta and lost its old lustre. Plato repeatedly pondered entering politics. His first great opportunity occurred during the reign of thirty tyrants, puppet pro-Spartan oligarchic government, among whose members were also Plato's relatives Critias and Charmides. Plato, however, was quickly disappointed by the new and harsh conditions. The second great opportunity appeared after the overthrow of tyranny and re-establishment of democratic conditions. But in 399, Socrates, "the justest man of that time" (Plat. *Ep*. 324e)[1] was condemned

---

[1] More important authors use the specific and universal custom to refer to the works. Plato used the so-called Stephanus numbers that are mentioned in the margins of the editions of Plato's works. Similarly, the so-called Bekker number is referred to in the works of Aristotle. At the same time each work has its own specific abbreviation (in this case the abbreviation Ep. It corresponds to Plato's *Letters*, *Epistulae*). Such

and so disillusioned that Plato turned away from politics for the second time. In the *Seventh Letter* he writes: "At last I came to the conclusion that all existing states are badly governed and the condition of their laws practically incurable, without some miraculous remedy and the assistance of fortune... and that the ills of the human race would never end until either those who are sincerely and truly lovers of wisdom come into political power, or the rulers of our cities, by the grace of God, learn true philosophy." (*Ep.* 326a-b). Thus after his political disappointments Plato brings up the idea of the philosophical foundations of a city, which has to come into existence by – even according to his own opinion – the very unlikely scenario of a government of philosophers who dedicate their lives to policy or politicians devoted to philosophy. With this opinion he takes several trips to Syracuse in Sicily. There he meets young Dion, who enthuses about philosophy and Plato's political thinking and together they tried to influence the governance of a local tyrant Dionysius II. Their attempts ended in failure and cost the life of Dion. Between trips to Syracuse Plato returned to Athens,

---

reference system is very practical, because the reader is not reliant on just one edition of the work of the classics, but he can browse for relevant passage in any issue that uses such pagination. For the official abbreviations of the selected writings of ancient and medieval authors see Porubjak-Vydra, 2008 or for the abbreviations of Plato's works Vydra, 174-175.

where he founded the Academy, a school of philosophy that lasted until 529 AD. Plato died in 347, supposedly on his birthday.

Among the sources that influenced the thinking of Plato, Socrates is undoubtedly in first place. But the poets Epicharmus and Pindar also influenced him, and in his thinking he follows Parmenides, whose vision of the eternal and unchanging being underpins the concept of the key ideas in Plato's times. During his travels he acquired knowledge of Pythagorean philosophy and many Pythagoreans were his friends, let us mention at least Archytas of Tarentum. Pythagorean influence is seen not only in his myths about the soul, but also in cosmology.

2. Work

Plato is the first author in the history of philosophy, whose works are preserved "first-hand" and to a significant extent. But his writings are atypical due to the fact that he refused to write "tracts" and instead he preferred the developed genre of the dialogue. Before we explain his motivation for this method of writing, we will briefly introduce some of his works chronologically.

Throughout his life Plato developed a dialogic form of writing in both style and content and based on that his works are usually divided into three periods. The determination of the period in view of the dialogue, as well as the chronology is still an open problem, but at least it has the advantage that it provides the reader with a particular primary orientation. In the first period we are talking about there were, the early, or *Socratic dialogues* and they included the *Defence of Socrates, Crito, Euthy-*

phro, Protagoras, Gorgias, or *Meno.* As the name suggests, the main protagonist is Socrates. The theme usually touches a variety of ethical issues, such as skills (*Arete*)[2] and whether they are teachable, or the question of the "assessment" (definition) of individual skills (piety, justice, moderation, etc.). A characteristic feature is that the debate between the protagonists often ends up in Aporia. We should not forget that there Plato already deals with issues of learning and recollection (*Meno*).

The second, the *middle period* of dialogues, manifests a greater thematic complexity and later, based on that, a "textbook" understanding of Plato developed as a so-called objective idealist, who held the theory of "two worlds." The reason is that Plato distinguishes between ideas as eternal, unchanging, and perfect beings and that perceived by the senses that are their imperfect imitations. So, the middle period thematically focuses on issues of discipline, which would later be called metaphysics, while

---

2   Greek expression *areté* is usually translated as "virtue." Several authors, however, point out that arête is hardly translatable and "virtue," as it has moral and ethical connotations, was wholly not involved in the original meaning. Although moral connotations are understandable, according to the Greeks, even natural things and artifacts could have *areté*. Therefore, the first translation of "efficiency" is more popular. *Arete* is a subjective expression in the superlative form of the adjective *agathos*, good. It is therefore a kind of best condition. A thing has arête if it does best, what it is for, such as a pen is efficient, if it writes well.

these issues are closely intertwined by various problems of knowledge, ethics, and politics. A typical example of the intertwining of the areas of interest is the *Republic*, where the main problem of justice is set not only in the context of ethical and political thinking, but overall philosophical view. Moreover, we include dialogues such as *Symposium, Phaedo,* or *Phaedrus* in this period.

The third period is made up of later dialogues in which Plato deepens and problematises many moments of earlier thinking. In the dialogue *Parmenides* he expresses serious objections to the theory of ideas. In the dialogue *Timaeus* he presents his cosmological concept and we should not omit Plato's longest work the *Laws*, where he revises some of his earlier conclusions regarding policy, particularly that mainly laws should govern cities.

An important question is why Plato prefers writing through dialogues and deliberately avoids prose.[3] From a philosophical treatise such as Aristotle's *Nicomachean Ethics* and Kant's *Critique of Pure Reason*, we expect that the author will give us his opinion and that defined in them we find "his" philosophy. This assumption, however, fails when reading Plato's dialogues and it is a frequent mistake that the reader takes them as a "doctrine," which is mediated by the authority of the person of the

---

[3] For details, see a great introduction to reading Plato's dialogues penned by J. Peterman (Peterman 2002) and chapter Plato's anti-tragic theatre in Nussbaum, 2,001

protagonist, most often by Socrates and takes it literally. In many parts of Socrates' works it is possible to find intentional sophistic arguments, free explanations of the matter or problem through myth or not entirely accurate analogies.

What is Plato's motivation for writing this way? We can see them by considering the written criticism of a text from the dialogue *Phaedrus* (Phaedr. 274b-277a). In this dialogue Socrates presents the myth of the Egyptian god Theuth and the king Thamus. God made several inventions, and among them he invented writing. When he presented his discovery to Thamus, the king asked him why it was important. Theuth believed that writing would help people to remember more. However, the king is more reserved, written words do not help us to remember inwardly, in our soul, but only outwardly. Among other objectors Socrates criticises the texts "The offsprings of painting stand there as if they are alive, but if anyone asks them anything, they remain most solemnly silent. The same is true of written words. You'd think they were speaking as if they had some understanding, but if you question anything that has been said because you want to learn more, it continues to signify just that very same thing forever." (275d-e). Socrates points out that the written text is something secondary and outward, it is a creation emanating from the soul of the author, where the interpretation is initially situated and where also lives the understanding of the certain thing that is interpreted in the text. Text is locked and inanimate, it is silent and therefore it cannot be asked and if it is criticised it cannot defend itself. It can be written only by its author. As an expert in a particular field has more knowledge about the topic than can be fit into the published volumes, the author has more on his mind than he puts into the text. In addition, the text is the same for everyone, although people are different and the same method of interpretation is not suitable for everyone. A good teacher who understands his subject well and knows his students can adapt his interpretation according to them. If he has only beginners he will not talk to them as to equal professionals, but if his students are advanced he can make greater demands in the interpretation and can also recognise that in some cases any explanation is useless, because the students do not have the ability to understand it. Silent and lifeless, the written text cannot adapt to the diversity of students as a teacher of flesh and blood can.

However, the preference of dialogue to academic prose is advocated by a further significant fact that he presents in the seventh of his *Letters*. Plato in rather sharp, but also mysterious language notes that he had never written any philosophy, and he who does so, is according to him a dilettante in this area: "So much at least I can affirm with confidence about any who have written or propose to write on these questions, pretending to a knowledge of the problems with which I am concerned, whether they claim to have learned from me or from others or to have made their discoveries for themselves: it is impossible, in my opinion, that they can have learned anything at all about the subject. There is no writing of mine about these matters, nor will there ever be one. For this knowledge is not something that can be put into words like other sciences" (Plat. Ep. VII, 341c). In other words, according to Plato, there are doctrines that have their objectives clearly defined and they may be interpreted. But in philosophy a full interpretation it is not possible, because the essence of philosophy, its own subject, cannot be expressed. Therefore it makes no sense to provide any interpretation. Yet this does not mean that this subject (in the *Republic* it is called the Good) gives no insight into our soul. The insight is the objective that may be obtained after a long effort of self-criticism and dialogue between an understanding teacher and pupil, who longs for understanding. This theme is also the background for written dialogues and Plato uses a variety of literary means to bring us closer to this insight.

Although the dialogue is also written in text, as opposed to treatise it provides a more liberal space to mimic live interview. Plato uses various tools to achieve his goals. First, the characters are of great importance. They have their origin, past, and not least a unique psychological character. Plato reflects these features in their opinions, their prejudices and biases. For some of them the gates of philosophy are closed for good (e.g. Anytos in the dialogue *Meno* or Kallikles in *Gorgias*) and they are satisfied with their own opinions and they do not want to critically examine them. Others have the ability to be open to philosophy, but the knowledge gained in the past prevents them from doing so (Menon in the eponymous dialogue). This is related to the second moment, which is often the aporeticism especially in early dialogues. Aporia, contradiction, is not a sophistic subterfuge here. The reason why they often do not get clear answers to these questions in dialogues lies in the fact that Plato provides a particular criticism of certain positions and attitudes that are unclear and controversial, but under normal circumstances their holders are unable to admit it. Since we consider our mistakes as something true, they do not show us reality. Therefore, before we start our own philosophical examination, it is necessary to "cleanse" ourselves from prejudices and untruths. Aporia, into which Socrates tries to bring his co-debaters; and which eclectically refutes their uncritically accepted opinions, purifies them; so they are open to issues and problems with their alleged truths burned to the ground.

Understanding then that the objective of philosophy starts with criticism and self-criticism to let a man be open to examination and new questions. In addition to Aporia and elenchi (disproving) Plato often relies on myths and analogies. The reason lies again in the nature of the reader. Philosophical understanding is the result of a long process in which the man is constantly exposed to questions and critical examination of his answers. We mentioned that the actual subject of philosophy, of which insight is the result, cannot be expressible in speech. Therefore, his immediate clarification for which the man might not be ready, would be quite similar to the attempt to describe the beauty of the colour red to a blind man. So Plato's only possibility is to clarify this subject indirectly via analogies which do not completely express his points, but at least approach them and draw our attention to it, as we see for example in the sun analogy.

In particular myths, if we take them literally, become the subject of misinterpretation. Their interpretation is usually free, they do not offer clear and distinct arguments and it is a mistake of the reader if they perceive them in that way. *Mythos* is not the same as the *logos*, but they have certain features in common. Both of them are some kind of speech, but *logos* is more associated with true knowledge. Compared to logos the myth is more ambivalent. If it claims an uncritical acceptance it becomes a source of errors. Therefore, Plato is a sharp critic of the traditional myth as a source of knowledge (for example, the dialogue Ion). However, he uses the myth himself, especially when he needs to turn our attention to something that is important and that escapes our attention. The myth is, like the analogy, appropriate if we can move closer to insight.

3. Concept of the Idea

Plato's concept of an idea is not entirely clear, even though it is one of the central terms. The background to this confusion is the fact that we have been meeting it since the early dialogues, though Plato continued to reflect and thematise it during various periods. Therefore, taking into account the scope of a period and a particular dialogue, we can distinguish different understandings of the concept of ideas. Etymologically, the expression "idea," like "shape" (*eidos*) has its origin in the expression "see," respectively in the form of aorist *idein*. Therefore an idea is represented by what is "seen," it is a definite "form" of things according how we distinguish them. But according to Plato an idea does not represent what we can see with our eyes, but with reason (cf. Kratochvíl, 143).

In early dialogues an idea corresponds to 'assessment' or the *definition* of something. So Socrates asks

Euthyphro in the eponymous dialogue: what is (*ti esti*) piety. The answer should clarify the idea of piety, i.e. give its definition. If a person has knowledge of something, she can express its idea. Socrates mentioned his expectations for the interpretation of assessment as follows: "So tell me now... is the pious not the same and alike in every action, and the impious the opposite of all that is pious and like itself, and everything that is to be impious presents us with one form or appearance in so far as it is impious?" (*Euthyphro*. 5c-d). In other words, there are a variety of acts that can be called impious and sinful, such as negligent homicide, murder, or theft. In contrast, there are a number of acts that appear pious such as prayer, sacrifice to the gods, etc. Whereas all these actions are called pious and their opposites impious, they have some common characteristics, which is the same and identical for all of them and it corresponds to the idea of the identity of piety or impiety. Thus to express the idea of piety means to give a general definition, which will be valid for all the specific cases of pious behaviour and things. The idea also has an important ethical significance because it has an important function as a paradigm (*paradeigma, Euthyphro*. 6e), according to which we can guide our actions. If Socrates had known what was pious and impious he would have known to live his life accordingly and avoid sin.

In the middle period dialogues the idea of the topic is further deepened. From the previous period remains the distinction between individual things that are many and their one abstract idea. The ideas here take the ontological status of perfect, eternal, simple, being graspable by reason as opposed to many, sensually perceptible things that are complex and subject to creation and destruction. Based on this distinction Plato developed the so-called theory of two worlds, the world of perceivable, dispensable things and the world of simple and eternal ideas that are isolated from each other by separation (chórismos). As we shall see, this view does not place sufficient emphasis on the bond (syndesmos) between ideas and things.

In some dialogues, the issue becomes the relation between ideas and sensually perceivable things. Already in the dialogue *Phaedo* Plato speaks about the presence (*Parousia*) of ideas in things, about the participation (*Methexis*) of things in ideas or about reciprocal communion (*koinonia*) (cf. Graeser, 191). *Chórismos* cannot be full; otherwise we would not understand the perceived reality at all. Basically, without "forms" we could not identify the individual objects, reality would be total chaos for us. In the late dialogue *Timaeus* Plato explicitly characterises the *cosmos*, the world as one, made by god according to the model of ideas, that is a unity of the unchanging divine spirit (*nous*), immortal, but the moving soul of the world (*psyche tú kosmú*) and a material body (*Tim.* 30a-c). In the later dialogues, particularly in the *Parmenides*, serious objections to the theory of ideas appear.

4. Anamnésis and Knowledge[4]

We begin the outline of Plato's thinking with the issue of *recollection, anamnesis*, which is a key concept of his theory of knowledge. For the first time we meet *anamnésis* in Plato in his dialogue *Meno*. The starting point for the clarification of recollection is the situation of Aporia to which Socrates introduces Meno, since he cannot answer the question, what is efficiency? Aporia has an important meaning here. This is not a sign of Socrates's sophistic superiority. To one who finds himself in aporiahis ignorance becomes apparent, or it turns out that their opinion (*doxa*) was only seemingly correct. Therefore the uncovering of contradictions in our thinking is of particular importance for it shows opinions as preju-

---

[4] To the problem of *anamnésis* see the article of Porubjak, 2008b, which I relate to.

dices that prevent us from searching for what is true and correct. Or in other words, if our opinion affirms what we know is true, we do not need to search and consider whether it is really so. Uncovering contradictions in opinions can relieve us from the negative effects of the opinion.

In the case of Meno the unveiling of contradictions in his attitudes, developed into the loss of speech. For in his discovered ignorance he is made as a fossil and this is why in a famous part of the dialogue he compares Socrates to a sea ray. For that fish fossilises its victims as Socrates causes silence and fossilisation uncovering the reputed knowledge. Meno says:

> "Indeed, if a joke is in order, you seem, in appearance and in every other way, to be like the broad torpedo fish, for it too makes anyone who comes close and touches it feel numb, and you now seem to have had that kind of effect on me, for both my mind and my tongue are numb, and I have no answer to give you. Yet I have made many speeches about virtue before large audiences on a thousand occasions, very good speeches as I thought, but now I cannot even say what it is." (*Meno* 80a-b).

Note that Meno is not an uneducated person. On the contrary, he is a talented young man and a student of the sophist Gorgias, who quite often talks about virtue. He knew various opinions; he knew something about argumentation, etc. In other words, Meno is already a person with *experience*.[5] Nevertheless, he does not have knowledge because he cannot answer the fundamental question.

By bringing Meno to aporia Socrates was able to start to the examination together, and thus search for the right answer about virtue. Meno, however, condemns this possibility of examination to failure:

> "How will you look for it, Socrates, when you do not know at all what it is? How will you aim to search for something you do not know at all? If you should meet with it, how will you know that this is the thing that you did not know?"(*Meno* 80d).

The possibility of examination is challenged by the argument that we cannot find a true answer if it is previously unknown. Although if we found it, according to Meno, we could not know that we have found what we were looking for. That is why Meno's argument makes any examination impossible in advance.

Nevertheless, Socrates wants to continue with the examination and to persuade Meno he starts a challenging project with him, he tells him a myth of recollection.

---

5   The notion of experience was for the Greeks wider than is typical in modern philosophy. It includes not only experience acquired through sensory perception, but also includes more complex units such as the views or opinions that can also be "heard" in words.

Therefore the myth has to refer to the reasonableness of examination, even if we are in a state of ignorance. Socrates assumes that the soul is immortal and therefore not even at the moment of death is it extinguished but travels to Hades. Here it serves its punishment for sins that were committed during life and after the completion of this punishment it returns. This is exactly where the soul gains knowledge:

> "As the soul is immortal, has been born often, and has seen all things here and in the underworld, there is nothing which it has not learned; so it is in no way surprising that it can recollect the things it knew before, both about virtue and other things. As the whole of nature is akin, and the soul has learned everything, nothing prevents a man, after recalling one thing only—a process men call learning—discovering everything else for himself, if he is brave and does not tire of the search, for searching and learning are, as a whole, recollection (*anamnésis*)" (*Meno* 81c-d).

Similar moments can also be seen in the myth of the charioteer from the dialogue *Phaedrus* (545b-557b). Here, also, an immortal soul dwells in the heavenly realm where it inspects the ideas. For the soul of a man is not as perfect as God, the influence of lust comes into the body and he then forgets about the inspection of ideas. According to Plato we are already born with knowledge, but when entering into the body, we forget it. Cognition is thus a recollection of what we saw before we were born. Other "textbook" interpretations, however, do not respect that in recognising that we have to rely on previous sensory experience. Several passages in the dialogues state the opposite:

> "But a soul that never saw the truth cannot take a human shape, since a human being must understand speech in terms of general forms (*eidos*), proceeding to bring many perceptions (*aisthéseón*) together into a reasoned (*logismó*) unity. That process is the recollection (*anamnésis*) of the things our soul saw when it was traveling with god, when it disregarded the things we now call real and lifted up its head to what is truly real instead." (*Phaedr.* 249b-c).

Our soul is born with knowledge and is therefore in itself a kind of idea. Without them we would not actually understand what we perceive, it would only be chaos and disorder for us. For example, we can perceive a lot of specific chairs, but the fact is that we recognise them is thanks to a kind of "chair" imprinted into our soul. Since we forget this knowledge, we are normally not aware of these kinds of ideas in our soul. Their awareness occurs precisely because of the perception given to us by specific things, and those we unify in generic terms.

In *Meno* Plato distinguishes opinion from knowledge. The first difference is that opinion can be correct (*orthé doxa*), but also incorrect. But knowledge can be only correct. Incorrect knowledge is not possible; it is *contradictio in adiecto*, a contradiction. But opinion also differs from knowledge in the following essential respect: knowledge is permanent and unchanging, while Socrates compared opinion to the mythical Daedalus' statues that were, as alive, and did not stand in one place (*Meno* 97d). Similarly, opinion is not fixed, but is subject to change. What Socrates has in mind, we can present with an example. A doctor is characterised by having knowledge of the human body and so he can well determine what is best for a sick person. But the sick person could choose to be cured by a charlatan who only presents himself as a doctor. Both doctor and quack will justify their actions differently, but since the patient is not educated in medicine, he cannot determine alone which one is truly better. In other words, he has only an opinion in this area and it may vary according to whose acts of justification are more convincing. At first he may hold the correct opinion, if he trusts in the processes of a real doctor, but it may change if the practices of a charlatan seem more appropriate.

Because opinion is unstable and changeable, Socrates proposes to bind it by means of the interpretation of causes (*aitias logismos*) and this bond by causes represents knowledge in the literal sense. In other words, knowledge can be defined as the *correct opinion that it is justified by the explanation of causes* (*Meno* 98a). Although the patient is unable to decide which of the two doctors is real, the true doctor should be able to identify a charlatan because the apparent healer does not know the true causes of physical phenomena, disease, and health. Therefore the apparent doctor does not convince him that he really knows how to heal. The doctor's knowledge is a justified correct opinion and is permanent and irreversible. Therefore, it is not enough to hold only opinions; we must strive for knowledge and thus justify our opinions. This distinction is also important for practical actions. We can consider either correctly or incorrectly what efficient actions are like and what efficiency is. A person who has the correct opinion about efficiency will act the same way as the one who knows efficiency, but this opinion is volatile. Having knowledge means to know what the efficiency itself is and knowingly makes it the cause of the correct action.

5. Plato's Analogies

We have mentioned that Plato used in dialogues analogies in order to turn our attention to something important or essential, which we normally do not see. Analogies do not show us meaning directly, but indirectly: they reveal the unknown through certain images that are better known to us. Therefore an analogy assumes a listener or reader who has some previous experience. The presupposition of the analogy is that it brings together an identity and a difference between the two things, because similar things are not quite the same nor completely different. Similarly, analogies are always characterised by common features in spite of differences.

a) The Sun Analogy
The core of Plato's thoughts can be outlined by three known analogies of the sixth and seventh books of the

Republic. They are the analogies of the sun, line, and cave. These analogies together form a whole and mutually refer to each other. The central theme of the *Republic* is justice and the analogies were preceded by a discussion about the fundamental powers that shape justice in the city, as well as in the individual. As Socrates' friends object, one key issue – the problem of the Good – remained unanswered. Socrates notes that he does not speak directly about what Good is, but first he presents his opinion of what appears to be a child of Good, opening the analogy of the sun (*Resp.* 506e).

Socrates starts his interpretation by differentiation:

"We say that there are many beautiful things and many good things, and so on for each kind, and in this way we distinguish them in words... And beauty itself and good itself and all the things that we thereby set down as many, reversing ourselves, we set down according to a single form of each, believing that there is but one, and call it "the being" of each... And we say that the many beautiful things and the rest are visible but not intelligible, while the forms are intelligible but not visible." (*Resp.* 507b-c).

Thus, at the beginning Socrates distinguishes between many phenomena and things that we call beautiful and their idea of good and beauty that is their only essence. While we perceive diverse phenomena by sensory perception, such as vision, we perceive ideas only by reason. In other words, in the world there are many sculptures and paintings that we call beautiful, but above them is the idea of beauty, of which there is only one and it forms the basis of everything we refer to as "beautiful." While paintings and sculptures are perceived visually, we see beautiful ideas only by reason. At first glance this differentiation might favour a "textbook" theory of two worlds, namely the conceivable world, on one hand, and the perceptible world, on the other. But Socrates does not speak about the world, but about visible areas (*topos horatos*) and imaginable areas (*topos noetos*). These are two diverse aspects of one world, not two separate worlds.

Subsequently Socrates proceeds to further differentiation. Two components are present for each perception: a *sentient* component and a *perceived* component. By vision (sentient component) we see colours (perceived component), by hearing we hear sounds, smell scents, and so on. But vision is different from the other senses, because for visual perception we need a third component, the *light* that makes things visible to the vision, and thus creates a kind of bond between them: "Then it isn't an insignificant kind of link that connects the sense of sight and the power to be seen—it is a more valuable link than any other linked things have got, if indeed light is something valuable" (*Resp.* 507e-508a).

However, light does not exist by itself, but it has its cause in something more superior, in the sun. Socrates notes that there is a certain affinity between the sun and sight: although they are not the same, sight can perceive only due to the fact that it accepts bursts from the sun and that allows him not only to perceive perceptible things, but also the sun itself. Without the sun as a *cause* of light sight would be burnt-out and it would be similar to blindness.

So far Socrates presented some picture, but only now he expresses its meaning by analogy. The *sun is a child of the Good,* mentioned at the beginning of the analogy, "which the good begot as its analogue. What the good itself is in the intelligible realm, in relation to understanding and intelligible things, the sun is in the visible realm, in relation to sight and visible things"(*Resp.* 508b-c). By labelling the sun as the child of the Good he points to a specific relationship between them. The Good is something more than the sun, it is its "father"(*Resp.* 506e), the originator and cause and therefore, something more dignified and more sophisticated than the child. It is natural, that the father rules over his child, not vice versa. But between a parent and a child is a "family" resemblance, analogy. As the sun allows the eye to see sensible things and the sun itself, then analogously (based on kinship) the Good allows us to "see" ideas, as well as good itself through reason. Without the Good our reason would be idle, because it could not inspect the eternal being. Thus as the Good is more superior and more dignified than the sun, so reason and the ideas that are grasped by reason, are more dignified than sight and perceive many diverse phenomena.

Socrates, however, develops the analogy further. As the sun gives us light, the Good gives us *truth* and thus enables knowledge. And such as light is the condition of the possibility for sight to see, thus truth is a condition of the possibility to be able to identify by reason. Therefore truth does not lay in reason, it is neither a compliance of things and reason (*adequatioreietintellectus*), but enables this compliance. However, the sun is not only the cause of light; but it gives things "origin, growth and nutrition, although it is not itself the origin" (*Resp*. 509b). Analogously to it the Good gives us *existence*. And as the sun is above light and growth, but it does not arise and grow, the idea of Good is the cause of truth and in some way more superior, but it is not the existence and truth. The Good is located, as Socrates says, "beyond existence" (*epekeina tés úsias*). After this conclusion Glaucon ironically declares: "By Apollo, what a daemonic superiority!" (*Resp*. 509 b-c). Despite comical undertones Glaucon hit the nail on the head. According to Plato it is beyond human possibilities to accurately express what the Good is. Any definition can only concern something that exists, that has a being. But since the idea of the Good is superior, it escapes notice. Therefore it is not possible to speak about it directly, and for this reason Socrates is reluctant to state any definition or interpretation at the beginning of the analogy. It is possible to speak about the Good only indirectly at best, by means of analogy (cf. Wyller, 35).

Let's try to make a summary. Socrates distinguishes between the conceivable and visible areas. In the first of these there are ideas that are existence or essence (*úsia*) and perceived by reason. The second region is a region of things perceived by sensory perception. Above this region rules the sun that gives us light and thus makes things visible to our sight. At the same time it gives us the possibility of origin, growth and nutrition, therefore it is the cause of perceptible things. Analogously to it, over the conceivable area rules the Good that gives us truth and existence. By means of truth it "illuminates" ideas for our mind, and thus allows knowledge. The Good, however, stands beyond existence and truth, and thus it is not possible to adequately express knowledge. It is evident that the structure is *hierarchical*. Conceivable and visible are not separated, but there is a kinship between them. Therefore the Good does not rule only over the conceivable region, but as the cause of the sun it is the cause of the visible.

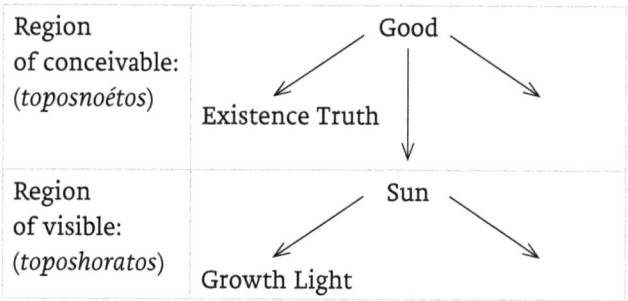

b.) The Analogy of the Line

After an indirect approach to the Good through the image of the sun, Socrates was invited by participants to develop his interpretation. Socrates responded with the analogy of the line (*Resp.* 509c-511e). In it he asks his friends to imagine a vertical line that he divided by unequal ratios (*logos*). From this division originate two unequally sized parts (I and II), corresponding to a visible and conceivable region that are further divided by the same ratio, so the result is an line consisting of four segments.

$$\begin{array}{c} \text{I.} \left[\begin{array}{c} \textit{Noéton} \\ \\ \textit{Aisthéton} \end{array} \right. \quad \begin{array}{c} \text{I.} \left\{ \begin{array}{c} A \\ B \end{array} \right. \\ \text{II.} \left\{ \begin{array}{c} C \\ D \end{array} \right. \end{array} \end{array}$$

The fact that the parts are divided by the same ratio has a symbolic significance, which is manifested in a mutual mathematical relationship between sections. It applies that the ratio of I: II is the same as the ratio of A: B, and then C: D. Moreover, it can be shown mathematically that the parts B and C are of the same size. We will see that Socrates is thus likely to outline the hierarchical structure of reality that is "mathematically" united under the *shared ratio, logos*, which together with the same size between sections B and C represent an important bond (*syndesmos*) between regions of the *cosmos* (cf. Wyller, 36-39).

Line also divides reality into the left and right parts. Therefore, as in the analogy of the sun, here we can also talk about the distinction between the way we grasp something and the grasped objects themselves. Based on that we can consider the left part as the area of the various stages of existence and the right as an area of stages of truth. The initial design of the line according to these divisions is as follows:

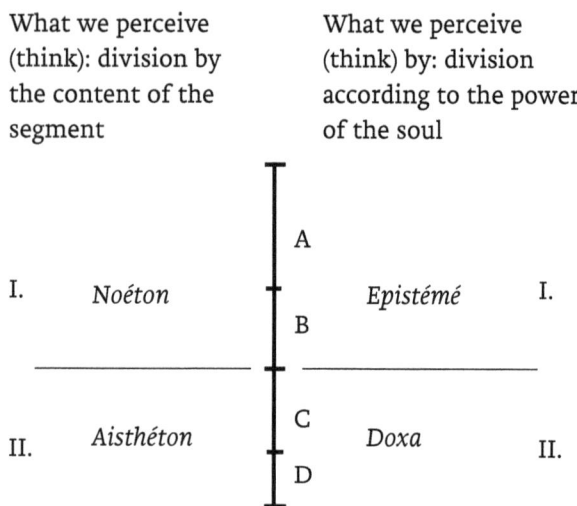

Region I (*noéton*) corresponds to the conceivable region and we grasp it through knowledge (*episteme*). Region II (*aisthéton*) corresponds to the visible region, it represents perceivable objects, which we grasp through opinion (*doxa*). This means that we can only have knowledge of what is eternal and unchanging; while we can only have an opinion about what is changeable. However, there is a specific proportional relationship between these regions. Since the *noéton* is higher in the hierarchy so those objects are more sophisticated and they exist "more" than objects of sense-perception. Analogously, knowledge has a higher dignity than opinion.

If to this preliminary sketch we add sections A – D, we get the final form of the line laid out in the table on the side 46.

Let's examine the individual sections. The perceivable region (*aisthéton*) is further divided into animate and inanimate things (C1) and to the area which is only their image, shadow, or picture (D1). Accordingly, we can also distinguish two ways of insight in the area of opinion. The first one is a kind of *estimation, eikasia* (D2), which refers to the "shadow of things." Above it is *belief, pistis* (C2) as a method of perceiving common things. *Pistis*, however, has little to do with faith in a religious meaning. As mentioned before, regarding the sensually perceptible things, according to Plato, we cannot have knowledge that is unchangeable such as its subjects are unchangeable. Sensory perceptible is changeable and

	Division according to the context of the section; "in terms of the stages of the records of existence"			Division according to the ability of the soul, "in terms of the stages of truth"		
	finer	basi		basic	finer	
A_1	ideas	**NOÉTON** perceived by mind	I	**EPISTÉMÉ** knowledge	*noésis* knowledge, understanding	A_2
B_1	mathematic, "natural" soundness				*dianoia*- thinking, deliberation	B_2
C_1	Ordinary "objects" animate and inanimate	**AISTHÉ- TON** perceivable by sense	II	**DOXA** opinion	*pistis* belief, faith, trust	C_2
D_1	Images of objects, pictures, shadows, visions				*eikasia* estimation, display	D_2

subject to creation and destruction, and thus we relate to it through opinion. Therefore Egil A. Wyller translates the term *pistis* aptly as to "consider-as-true"(Wyller, 43).

Pistis represents our most common attitude towards reality; it is about trust or the belief of how things generally behave. We can also see that the relationship between areas C and D is the same as that between sections I and II. Therefore, the shadows and images are something less than the animate and inanimate things and this is adequate to estimate the less perfect and less precise way of seeing than faith. Observing the shadow we simply acquire less accurate information than observing the thing that causes the shadow.

In the conceivable region (*noéton*) we see the differentiation between mathematical and natural patterns (B1) from ideas (A1) that are not explicitly mentioned by Socrates. We observe patterns through discursive thinking, *dianoia* (B2) until by the observation of ideas we reach a peak in the form of knowledge, *noesis* (A2).

How do *noesis* and *dianoia* differ? The level of observation of mathematical and natural patterns corresponds to science (*techné*) and a *par excellence* representation of science for the Greeks was geometry. According to Socrates a consideration is based on certain assumptions (*hypotheseis*) that are implicitly accepted as valid truths and are not examined further. Socrates explains, "I think you know that students of geometry, calculation, and the like hypothesize the odd and the even, the various figures, the three kinds of angles, and other things akin to these in each of their investigations, as if they knew them. They make these their hypotheses and don't think it necessary to give any account of them, either to themselves or to others, as if they were clear to everyone. And going from these first principles through the remaining steps, they arrive in full agreement"(*Resp.* 510c). In other words, a geometre, who faces the task to construct a certain shape, does not ask what is an line, a straight line or a triangle. The terms are clear to him. Therefore, he can proceed from axioms *directly* to the desired solution. Finally, *dianoia* can rely on sensory perceptible images and reproductions as a specific aid to better understand certain abstract patterns. A drawn circle or triangle is not a geometrical shape in the true sense for a mathematician. Triangles, circles, and straight lines exist only as conceivable objects (Patočka 2012, 42). But he can draw a right angle triangle to better understand Pythagoras' theorem and the necessary geometric relations that it affects. Thus *dianoia* is situated between opinion and reason (*nús*). Thus, we can summarise that Socrates in the analogy of the line talks about three features typical for discursive thinking: 1. uncritical *acceptance* of assumptions, axioms, 2. *directly proceeding* from assumptions to solution, 3. *helping by images* perceptible by the senses.

Noesis, knowledge and understanding, differs from *dianoia* at exactly these three points. This is the highest method of observation, its subject is what is complete and perfect and we reach it by means of *dialectic*. 1. It is a purely intellectual insight and therefore it does not rely on any aids from sensory images. 2. A dialectician proceeds from the same assumptions (*hypotheseis*) as a scientist (*technités*), but does not accept them as unproblematic. On the contrary, he heads away from them to the ideas that are their roots and through them to what "the unhypothetical first principle of everything (*pantos arché*)" (*Resp.* 511b). According to the analogy of the Sun we now know that this begins with the idea of the Good. 3. A dialectician thus does not reach the solution directly, but by a "detour" from the assumptions to their point of origin and then only subsequently to the solution of the problem. A dialectician therefore proceeds by two movements: he carries out *anabasis*, an ascent from the assumptions higher than the beginning, to subsequently undertake *katabasis*, the subsequent descent from these beginnings going lower to resolve the issue.

c) Analogy of the Cave

Ascending and descending movements also have an important *educational meaning* that Plato develops in the famous image of the cave enclosing and capping a trio of analogies in the *Republic*. Plato, with the picture of a prisoner emerging from the cave to the "normal" world and subsequently descending back, presents his vision of *paideia*, which is not just education, but rather rearing in the broad sense, of which an essential part is education. It is also a very apt criticism of the "normal" non-philosophical attitude, the life that does not examine itself, not only because of laziness, but because it believes that it "knows" the reality. Socrates outlines the bizarre image of prisoners in a cave who are tied, they cannot move, and therefore their sights are fixed on the wall opposite them. Behind them there is a fire illuminating the dark cave and between the fire and the prisoners is a small wall behind which jugglers do different performances and carry over it a variety of objects. Due to the light of the fire behind projected onto the wall in front of the prisoners they are a shadow play. Beyond this whole cluster there is an exit leading out of the cave.

Because the people in the cave look at the shadows before them all their lives, they do not consider them as the imitations of objects, but the real objects. Socrates continues that if anyone untied one of the prisoners, who would then be able to look around, he would inevitably be confused. For he was accustomed to only watch shadows in the dusk, direct sight into the light in the cave would blind him, his body would be stiff and movement would hurt him. If someone had told him that the objects carried by the jugglers over the wall are real, he would consider that person a fool. Here, it is important to highlight one moment. Quite often it is mistakenly believed that the prisoner breaks out on his own accord. The reality is exactly the opposite, a prisoner lives in the belief of the authenticity and veracity of what he sees all his life and therefore he has no reason to free himself. He does not know that the shadows are only imperfect copies of things and therefore he does not yearn to know more. Also for this reason, even after his bonds are untied he does not want to come out of the cave, and because of the pain and disorientation he wants to return to the primary oppression. So he does not abandon the cave by his own choice. Exactly the opposite, somebody has to get him out by force. But the prisoner's confusion remains, even outside the cave. He is painfully blinded by the glare of the sun so even here he fails to recognise different things (i.e. 515e-516a).

Change occurs only when his sight becomes accustomed to the new environment outside the cave by gradual observation of everything that is known to him until he will be able to adequately see and recognise the unknown: "At first, he'd see shadows most easily, then images of men and other things in water, then the things themselves. Of these, he'd be able to study the things in the sky and the sky itself more easily at night, looking at the light of the stars and the moon, than during the day, looking at the sun and the light of the sun ... Finally, I suppose, he'd be able to see the sun, not images of it in water or some alien place, but the sun itself, in its own place, and be able to study it" (*Resp.* 516a-b). A freed prisoner thus does not immediately see things as they are, but he relates them to the knowledge and experience gained in the cave (shadows), and he is able to recognise mirror images on the water. Only then he sees visible objects that cast shadows and are reflected on the water's surface. Without previous experience he does not perceive the sun as the cause of all perceivable, but first he sees the celestial bodies, stars and moon at night, that is under conditions that are similar to the gloom of the cave. Only then is he able to recognise the sun during the day, and finally "at this point he would infer and conclude that the sun provides the seasons and the years, governs everything in the visible world, and is in some way the cause of all the things that he used to see" (*Resp.* 516b-c).

After the former prisoner recognises the lawful orderliness of the visible region and how it is more perfect and more beautiful when compared to dwelling in the cave, he is sorry for the other prisoners, he goes back in order to tell them about that beauty and order. But because he descends from the place illuminated by the natural light of the sun into the gloom of the cave his eyesight is weakened again. He does not orientate himself in the cave as the others, and when he tells them what the world "up there" is like, he faces misunderstanding, mockery, and in the worst case he is even killed.[6] As we shall see, the depiction of the descent is more than just a demonstration of the alleged impracticality of the philosopher in "the real world." The reason for the unfortunate fate of the returnees lies not only

---

6   At this point Plato hints to the process and death of Socrates.

in the repeated disorientation in the cave environment, but especially in the fact that the others, given that they see only shadows all their lives, are unable to understand his vision. His cellmates, the same as our prisoner, when he got rid of his handcuffs, do not want to be freed.

When Glaucon remarks that the image of prisoners in a cave is strange, Socrates adds that they are "similar to us"(*Resp.* 515A). How? Let's note that the image of the cave apparently follows the analogy of the line, it moves in the perceptible region, which is the most famous area for us, where the sojourn in the cave corresponds to D and the area outside the cave to C. But the reference to the analogy of the sun is also apparent, whereas in both areas there is a source of light, in the form of fire in the cave and the sun outside the cave. As a prisoner leaves the cave moving from the familiar field towards the unknown, from the space where fire reigns to the area illuminated by the sun, thus Socrates asks us to ascend from simple opinion and the visible region (II) to the thinkable, to *epistémé* (I) until we reach the Good. In the cave, the prisoners consider shadows as something real; it is their normal, natural attitude to which they are accustomed. We are similar to them because we also consider what is visible as literally true. Socrates notes that the issue of looking for Good is a thorny and difficult path that lies in the continual critical examination of our experiences and ideas, until we reach the point where our soul suddenly (*exaifnés*) recognises the veracity and existence of a higher level and Good as its cause.

Let's return to the concept of *anabasis* and *katabasis* within the analogy of the line. Compared with the analogy of the sun and thus with the example of the line Plato develops and in detail outlines the hierarchical structure of reality. The terms *anabasis* and *katabasis* warn that on individual sections we can ascend and descend as on the "heavenly ladder"(Wyller, 45). Ascent from the section D1 to A1, that is, in the column of stages of existence is the ascent of what is numerous and exists as imperfect and uncertain, towards a more consistent, better and more apparent, from the multiplicity of sense-perceptible things to the unity of ideas, to the idea of Good as the beginning of everything. At the same time it is also about an *ascent in the hierarchical row of causes*. Shadows and images (D1) do not exist independently. They would not exist in the absence of animate and inanimate things (C1) that cast them and are thus are the causes of their origin. Since between sections C and D prevails the same ratio as between the conceivable (I) and perceptible (II) areas, conceivable is the cause of perceptible. Therefore, we can deduce that, as things would not exist without perceptible shadows and images, thus there were no perceptible things (C1) without natural and mathematical patterns (B1). Finally, neither numbers nor geometric shapes and other similar assumptions on which science is based, would not be possible for them if there were no ideas (A1) above them, for example the idea of unity and multiplicity. However, we can also talk about descent: the first beginnings of everything is the Good, and everything else, from ideas to shadows, emerge from it. It is a descent from the perfect to the imperfect, from single to multiple, from existence to what exists "less" and finally from the eternal to the dispensable. Based on that, shadows and images are some kind of border of existence, it cannot be said that they are nothingness, something non-existent, but they are the most distant from perfection of existence in the full sense of the word.

Anabasis and *katabasis* are carried out on the right side of the degrees of truth. The ascent proceeds from *eikasia*, from observing shadows that are rather nebulous, the least obvious and passes through the observation of perceivable things by means of *pistis* that has a lesser degree of non-conspicuity. *Eikasia* and *pistis* belong to the area of *opinion*. As indicated by the Analogy of the Cave, it is the most common and most widespread way of observation in which we are directed to previous experience of how things generally behave. But opinion, as we have mentioned, is changeable and unstable and is needs to be tied by the explanation of causes. This happens in science based on the thoughts, *dianoia*, which unlike opinion is an observation of eternal laws and rules, whereby with the help of dialectic reason can reach *noésis*. Plato's dialectic is thus trying to "export the best of the soul to the observation of the best in existence" (Gadamer, 58).

This method is not directly opposed to the traditional "textbook" interpretation, according to which the philosopher cuts himself off from previous experiences to observe the ideas. In the analogy of the cave, we could notice that the transition to seeing perceptible things was gradual, that our first prisoner relied on what he knew from the cave and only then, could he proceed higher. Analogously, nor are we in pursuit of acquisition of *dianoia* or *noesis and* cannot quite give up what we have already learned. However, the philosopher also undertakes the way down, he comes down from the heights of clarity and visibility into less perfect, less sharp observation, but during the descent, is aware that the *cosmos* is completely arranged in various sites, and the arrangement stems from the idea of the Good as the first beginning.

What is the educational meaning of the analogy of the cave, respectively three analogies as such? As we have mentioned above in connection to the *Seventh Letter*, Plato does not attempt to describe the very subject of philosophy, which is called the Good in the *Republic*, directly, as to present its explicit description is not possible. On the contrary, one who does so is only an apparent philosopher. There can be observed the root of Socrates' opposition to those who want to teach philosophy in this way and to educate: "Education is not in reality what some people proclaim it to be in their professions. What they aver is that they can put true knowledge into a soul that does not possess it, as if they were inserting vision into blind eyes"(*Resp.* 518b-c). Knowledge cannot hide in rolls and books, but reigns in the soul, which sees not only visually, but especially by reason. So it is presented in the soul, which mainly understands. Education, therefore, does not lie in the memorising of texts and precepts, but in converting the attention of reason, as a leading component of the soul, to what real is and the Good itself. From this it should be clear that this ascent to Good happens gradually. First we have to come to an observation that takes place in the sciences and if we understand their assumptions we are able to provide an adequate interpretation. However, the philosopher cannot simply donate the Good as a goal of rational observation through interpretation, but it may turn his student's attention to different sides, hoping his soul will suddenly "see."

6. Soul and City

Plato's understanding of the soul is not clearly given, and depending on dialogues we can find diverse and often contradictory claims. It concerns the core of Plato's thought, which links the problems of metaphysics and ontology with the problems of knowledge and ethics. Similarly, as with other important issues, in problems of the soul it is also based on analogies and myths. Nevertheless, we face a number of moments that stand (more or less) in general. Even with a problem of recollection we meet that, according to Plato, the soul is eternal, it does not arise and it does not expire. The Pythagorean influence is also seen in the idea of the cycle of reincarnation of the soul, as he outlines it in the myth about the charioteers in Phaedra. The soul is different from the body because of its immortality, which follows the Orphics presented as "a grave of the soul" (*Crat.* 400c), as a prison, which harasses us by its needs and so prevents us "in pursuit of being" (*Phaedo*. 66c). The contradiction between body and soul would encourage us to come to the conclusion, that concerning knowledge, we must turn away from the body by severe austerities. According to Plato, instead of a radically ascetic life it is sufficient if one leads a life of moderation and does not give his body more than it needs.

Plato also deals with the soul in the *Republic*, where he develops the famous analogy between the soul and community. Socrates in a discussion with Adeimant and Glaucon reaches a decision, that if they want to see what is a fair man is they must look for something bigger, for a fair community and then compare it to the man.[7] Since such a just city does not exist, it must first be "established" in the mind. Such a community would

---

7 Often in the context of the analogy between the soul and the community it is stated that, according to Plato, "the community is the man in capital letters" (for example Voegelin, 136), and we often may encounter this statement in quotes (even though our example above is an exception), what may encourage us to believe that it is a quotation. However, Plato does not speak like that in the Republic and thus the pronounced is a cliché that simplifies the overall problem of analogy. In the second book, Socrates notes that the question of the fair man "is not for a man with poor eyesight." Such people prefer to read first what is written in capital letters and only then, they read the same inscription in lowercase. In addition, because the participants of a dialogue together with Socrates have "low vision," he proposes to look first for

consist of three classes: producers, guardians, and philosophers-rulers. The class of producers is made up of peasants, artisans, merchants, and wageworkers. Their role is to nourish the community and provide goods for their basic needs. Above them stand guardians protecting the community against external conflicts and from internal dissension and strife. Highest in the hierarchy of the city stand just rulers, who are also philosophers. Therefore, Plato in the Republic outlines the known concept of the fair government of philosophers, which is perfect for all regimes and should end the misery of humankind arising because communities are not well organised (*Resp.* 473d-e).

Each of these classes is also attributed specific virtues (*aretai*). Rulers have *wisdom* (*sofia*), they are educated in philosophy and dialectics, and thus lead the community to a genuine good, not only to the apparent good and govern the city as a whole, not only in favour of their own class. Guardians on the other hand are characterised by courage (*andreia*), which lies in their ability to recog-

---

something bigger than a fair man is, and that is fair community. Only then is possible to proceed to the recognition of a fair person as an individual (*Resp.* II, 368C-369a). The above-mentioned "citation" leads us to overlooking the fact that the analogy between the community and the soul of man is only an approximation of Plato's consciousness. Regarding the problem of inaccuracies in this analogy see also Thein, 245-313.

nise what is to be feared and what is not. Socrates compares the guardians to faithful dogs who turn against the unknown, but listen to their master, that means to the class of rulers. The class of manufacturers is represented by the virtue of *moderation (sófrosyné)*. Moderate manufacturers are aware of their place in the community, they accept it and do not struggle against it, and they do not claim the position of guardian or rulers. *Justice* will prevail in the city when all of these virtues are present. In other words, justice is a total virtue, which includes all of the other virtues. Therefore, it does not belong to any of the classes separately, but it is the harmonising power of the community as a whole, which brings the various components of the city into harmony. In addition, Plato characterised justice as the ability to "do one's own," so avoid dedication to several activities at once *(polypragnomein, Rep.* 433a), for one has to do only what he is naturally best suited to do. Thus we get a quartet of virtues which later will be called *cardinal* (Aubenque 2003, 46). In addition, Plato also talks about the contradictions of virtues: *ignorance, cowardice, wantonness*, and finally the *injustice* that results from them (Resp. 609B-C). They obviously do not harmonise the community; they bring discord and strife. The city in which citizens do not carry virtues is a place of injustice and decline.[8]

---

8 Regarding the issue of civil virtue in Plato and Aristotle see Porubjak 2008.

After the founding of the fair city, Socrates with his friends starts to search for a just man. From Socrates' suggestion, that such a person will be similar to the just city, is raised the question whether the soul includes in itself any of the three ingredients, as the best city consists of three classes. In other words, one has to ask whether the soul is something homogenous, simple, solid, or a union of several different components. Socrates' reasoning is based on the mental conflict that he characterises as follows: "It is obvious that one single factor would not want to do the opposite and suffer several storylines simultaneously in respect of the same component and its relationship to the outside of being, so wherever we find that they are done, we know that it was not one factor, but more"(*Resp.* 336b-c). In other words, if the soul was whole and without components it could not, in relation to the same outer matter, want something and not want it at the same time. If we are thirsty and have a glass of water, we drink it. However, if we knew that the water in the glass is poisoned, there would be a conflict in our soul. Part of the soul would like to quench our thirst; another part would prevent us from doing so because drinking the glass of water would harmful. Thus, we can want and not want the same thing at the same time. Due to this mental ambivalence, it must be concluded that several components are present in the soul.

The first component is *lust (epithymétikon)*, which leads us to the fulfilment of our basic needs, such as satisfying hunger, thirst, sexual needs, and so on. The component, which resists the drinking of the poisoned water in our example, is *reason (logikon)*. However, Socrates recognises a third component *wrathfulness* or *valour (thymos)*, which is closely related to our need for self-esteem and is manifested, for example, when lust encourages us to do something shameful, but we are angry with ourselves that we ask for such a thing. Nevertheless, *thymos* is also closely related to the relationships with other people, to the way that other people see us. If we were concerned that our honour and esteem in the eyes of others would fall, that we would face public disgrace if we did something inappropriate, we would not do it. Thymos is thus a kind of emotional component, which manifests itself in feelings of anger as well as shyness or shame when we are dealing with honour and respect. This concept of the three components is called the *trichotomic* concept of the soul.

Like the best class in the city, the individual components of the soul have their specific functions. Obviously, there is tension between these functions; otherwise conflict between them would not be possible. For guidance in our life it is not irrelevant which component we prefer, because if either part dominates it guides the way the character of a man is formed. For example, if lust is dominant, reason succumbs to it and it serves as a tool to achieve shameful goals. In contrast, a person with a dominant component of valour is able to suppress lust due to his own ambitions and efforts to acquire honour and respect in the eyes of others.

Let us have a look at these components. The highest component is reason, which lies in the head but as the "smallest" component only seldom rules. By means of reason we can relate to eternal ideas and thoughts, and thus acquire knowledge and cultivate dialectic. People for whom reason is a more dominant component than valour and lust, acquire the virtue of wisdom and Plato calls them wisdom lovers, hence philosophers. Valour is a lower component and is an interface between reason and lust. According to his dialogue, *Timaeus* resides in the heart and is associated with feelings of anger, so it is a kind of emotional characteristic of a man. As long as *thymos* is adequately trained by education and allows itself to be guided by the intellect, it becomes an ally against lust and acquires the virtue of courage. Although it is not able to acquire knowledge, it can acquire the correct opinions. We have mentioned that *thymos* is a component inherent in social relations. As the dominant component it leads to the acquisition of honour, to assert itself in the struggle against others and fulfil their own ambitions at the expense of others. Plato called these people *victory lovers*. Lust indeed is the component of the lowest status, but it is usually in the most powerful and most often in the character of the ruler. Its seat is the liver and it is not able to acquire knowledge or opinion. It is just a sort of rather nebulous, repellent anticipation that aims at self-preservation. Although it is a component that is not rational, once it is disciplined it is able to listen to reason and adopt the virtue of moderation. People in whom lust is dominant are *profit lovers*.

We have mentioned that the soul of a man is a dynamic mix of tensions that arise between the different functions of its parts. This does not mean that they cannot harmonise reciprocally. If a class of philosophers has to rule the city, so reason has to rule over the soul, and its task is to guide the other components. Such a soul is not only smart, but also brave and last but not least moderate. Moreover, if these virtues dwell in it, it is fair and in balance with itself. Since each component has its natural function, none of them is bad, nor are the principle of evil. Without lust, we would not care for the preservation of life, without valour we would not value our self-esteem and we would not respect others. Non-virtue therefore lies in the fact that the individual components exceed the limit that naturally belongs to them, so a person follows the primary desires or has exaggerated ambitions.

Plato in the eighth book of the *Republic* further applies this dynamic of the soul to the differentiation of various political regimes. The only just regime is an *aristocracy* that is the government of the best (*aristoi*). It is a regime of ruler-philosophers whose government relies on reason. A less perfect form of government is *timocracy*, a government of honour that is installed by people in whom valour is dominant. Regarding lust, if it is dominant three types of constitution may arise. The first is the *oligarchy*, the government of the rich, whose instability lies in the fact that under its leadership, the differences between rich and poor are widened. Compared to it the lower form of government is *democracy*. This regime is egalitarian and it most values freedom, consisting of choice in the many ways of life. This freedom is imperfect, because it is not based on virtue. The wishes of the people are unstable, changing from day to day depending on their mood and improper political decisions also correspond to it supported by the populist rhetoric of "bad waiters" (Resp. 562d), who, in order to gain favour from the people, give unrealistic promises. The worst form of government is *tyranny* into which an untied democratic freedom leads. Towards the end of a period of democracy people require the fulfilment of unrealistic demands, which a tyrant uses to gain power. Since he is not then able to meet these expectations, he begins to govern through fear and violence, and thus from the most free regime comes the greatest oppression.

Aristotle

1. Life

Aristotle, the most significant of Plato's students, was born in 384 BC in the Macedonian city of Stagira, for this reason he is often referred to as The Stagirian. His father, Nikomachos, worked as a royal Macedonian physician; therefore, Aristotle himself had many connections in the Macedonian royal court. From a political and social point of view, it was a period of constant battles between the Greek cities. The disputes exhausted the towns and helped Macedonia rise to power. Therefore due to his birthplace, Aristotle's life was accompanied with political turbulence that directly concerned him. At the age of seventeen or eighteen, a young Aristotle came to Athens and joined Plato's Academy where he remained for twenty years. During that time, he acquired the reputation of being a profound thinker. In the meantime, Phillip II's rise to power in Macedonia caused a lot of discomfort in Athens, so Aristotle decided to leave the Academy. After his departure from Athens, he dedicated himself to diverse exploration and on the island of Lesbos he met Theophrastus, who became his friend and successor. In 343 BC, or 342 BC, Phillip II invited him to Macedonia to tutor his son Alexander, the future Alexander the Great, which of course, provoked mostly exaggerated speculation about his influence on Alexander's intentions to conquer. Aristotle's political thoughts were primarily based on the notion of the Greek polis, which is of restricted size and is supposed to create an environment to allow the individual abilities excel. In 335 BC Aristotle was allowed to return to Athens, where he established the Lyceum, a rival school to the Academy. This second period was also ended by an anti-Macedonian feelings that began after the death of Alexander in 323 BC. Aristotle was accused of impiety, and remembering the fate of Socrates in the autumn of his life he left Athens, remarking, "I will not allow the Athenians to sin twice against philosophy."

2. Work

The "life" of Aristotle's work is also significant. The most obvious difference between his works and Plato's dialogues is his writing style. Aristotle's work was an austere, strict, and acrimonious language that was difficult to grasp. Therefore the present-day reader is often surprised by Cicero's comparison of Aristotle's style to the river of gold (Shields). The reason for the difficulty of comprehension is that Aristotle's work was not completely preserved. Aristotle's works are divided into exoteric, i.e. meant for the public, and esoteric, compiled from his lectures, notes, papers, etc. The systematisation of the work of Aristotle by Andronicus of Rhodes is an important milestone and the reason why some texts survived. The reason for the difficulty of comprehension is that Andronicus excluded from the set of Aristotle's works his writings meant for the public, and that was why they were not preserved

Andronicus also played a significant role in another aspect. He organised Aristotle's work into more areas, giving the indirect impression of Aristotle's thoughts being systematic, coherent, and whole (Ricken, 86). As a matter of fact, until the 20th century there had been an approach to Aristotle's thinking as a unified and comprehensive concept, so the inconsistencies in his work were either overlooked or referred to as moments in which the author had no time to think "to the end."[9] Naturally, this makes interpretation even more difficult.

The first section of Aristotle's work is called *Organon* (meaning instrument, tool) and Andronicos included his works on logic, such as *Categories, Prior Analytics, Posterior Analytics, On Interpretation*, etc. In the work logics, Aristotle proposes a "tool" to conduct and rectify our thinking. Logic provides a formal procedure based on which from a true premise we can arrive at a true conclusion.

The second group consists, generally speaking, of works on physics such as movement, motion, creation

---

[9] An important response to this problem was a development concept from Werner Jaeger. According to him, the problems of irregularity arise from the fact that Aristotle's thinking developed during his life. Therefore, at a later period his opinions were contrary to his previous opinions. An interesting critique of the previously mentioned "systematic" approach is introduced by Pierre Aubenque (see Preface in Aubenque, 2014)

and destruction (e.g. *Physics*), biological research, studies of natural phenomena, or psychological concepts (*On the Soul*).

The third group is called *Metaphysics*. Aristotle never used this term; it was probably Andronicus' idea, which included his works following (*meta*) physics. However, this title turned out to be appropriate, since the main object is the most general inception and causes of immaterial being as such. It is a science that is more abstract and superior to physics, in other words, "beyond" physics.

The fourth group, and the most important nowadays, are the works on the practical philosophy of experience and practice. It includes works on ethics and politics, two tightly linked fields. According to Aristotle, political theory is a supreme discipline, because it is about the highest, pursuable good, the well-being of the community, and, consequently, of the individual, since he is part of the community (NE 1094a27-b13). Works belonging to this group are *Nicomachean Ethics*, *Eudemian Ethics*, *Magna Moralia*, *Politics*, and *Athenian Constitution*.

Finally, there are the poetic works that focus on literary theory (*poiésis*), such as *Rhetoric*, about the composition of speech, or *Poetics*, about poetry and drama. The rest of the group is fragments that are not preserved in any other form (e.g. *Protreptikos*).

3. *Organon* and the Theory of Cognition

We begin our approach to Aristotle's theory with a brief introduction as to how we acquire knowledge. This reflects his empiricism. According to Aristotle, human beings have a natural craving for knowledge as demonstrated by the predilection for sensual perception, in particular sight. We want to learn for the sake of knowledge itself, not for any other reason (*Met.* 982b20). We come to this world without any previous knowledge; we are born as blank slates (*tabula rasa*) that start to fill up after encountering particular, individual things. Although we do not possess an inborn knowledge, thanks to our senses, memory, and mind, we have a natural disposition to acquire it. Through the senses, we receive perceptions, which are saved in memory. Since it stores more than one perception, it can find similarities and create experiences. According to Aristotle, the way of acquiring knowledge is *inductive,* i.e. generalising from particular cases.

Experience is not actual knowledge, or more precisely, it is not a science. That is because a specific skill or art (*techné*) and knowledge (*epistémé*) are the recognition of the causes of the phenomenon. Science answers the question "why." Experience itself does not provide us answers; at most, it tells us "what" things are, not "why" they exist. Based on experience we know that a fire is hot, but we do not know the cause (energy released by an object that burns). An expert is expected to know the cause, and not to have just experienced it.

Scientific cognition is based on logic. As it was mentioned before, *organon* means "tool, instrument." Logic is not a science, but it is an essential tool to systematise individual notions and properly relate them. To enable this, science needs clear concepts that are consecutively combined into sentences. According to the basic formal standards, it is possible to make real conclusions from sentences and premises, provided are all true. Concepts are obtained thanks to the hierarchical classification of words, from specific to general. Aristotle calls the specific term "species" (*eidos*, lat. *species*), and the general term that refers to several classes, "genus" (*genos*), whereby specific concepts often tell us more about the thing than general concepts:

"For example, if we wish to speak about a man, we make it clear by saying: it is a man, instead of referring to him as a living being. While species can be common for various objects, genus indicates what is distinctive about a man. It is also more definitive to name a tree "tree" instead of a "plant" (*Cat.* 2b8-2b22).

Nevertheless, general terms are important because they allow us to define the concepts accurately and express them properly. We could get the definition by assigning the species to the genus (*genus proximum*), but that is not enough. For example, if we want to define a man, it is not sufficient to say he is a living being, because that genus consists of many species. We need to find a distinctive feature that belongs only to the species we wish to define. For a human being, this feature is: has a mind, so the definition of man is "thinking living being" (*zoóon logon echon*). Let us give an example of an inaccurate definition. It could be: "a man is a creature with two legs." Although bipedalism is characteristic for men, it is not a unique characteristic, since apart from human beings there are other two-legged animals (for example birds). The error consists of the assignation of a characteristic to only men, when it is also typical for other species of the genus "animal."

Not everything is definable, categories and specific things are the exception. Categories are so called supreme genus, the most general concepts. They are impossible to characterise because there is nothing more abstract than their definition. A specific thing is, on the other hand, a *tode ti*, literally "this here," which can be pointed at. For that reason, we can only define general genus and species that are ranked between categories and individual things in the linguistic hierarchy.

If we want to define a concept, we can incorporate in a premise formed by a subject and a predicate. As we mentioned before, if we have true premises, based on formal structures, we can come to a true conclusion. In this case, the valid linguistic hierarchy enables deduction, i.e. a method to deduce a specific conclusion from general statements, the opposite of induction. We explain it with a common example. We have two premises: "All human beings are mortal" and "Socrates is a human being." The former refers to a general characteristic of all humans – each and every human being is mortal. The latter mentions a specific man, Socrates. The term "human being" represents the connection between the two premises. Since Socrates is a human being, he will share the characteristics of all humans, consecutively, if every human is mortal, Socrates has to be mortal, too.

In the same way that indefinable concepts exist, there are also sentences that are impossible to prove by deduction, such as the Principle of Non-Contradiction and the Principle of Excluded Middle. The former means that a certain attribute cannot at the same time apply and not apply to the same subject (*Met.* 1005a19-20). In other words, it is not possible for a particular premise to be true and not true at the same time. On the other hand, the Principle of Excluded Middle (Met. 1011b20) says that one of two contradicting premises has to be true. From a logical point of view there is no third option, a middle way. It is impossible to prove these principles, but all proof is based on them and presumes them (*Met.* 1006a ff.).

We have mentioned that we gain to knowledge inductively. What meaning then does logic and deduction have? We can talk about knowledge as if it is true. Truth at the same time does not lie in things, but in judgments. For example, if we claim that every triangle is right-angled, by logical deduction it is easy to prove that we are mistaken, because we can show that also acute and obtuse triangles exist. Therefore, logic and deduction also have an important controlling role and enable us to reveal and to correct mendacity. This is particularly important in the struggle against sophistic arguments that intentionally abuse the vagueness of concepts as well as the breach the principle of dispute.

An important contribution to logic, by which we stand on the threshold of metaphysics, is the science of categories. Aristotle distinguished ten categories: substance, quantity, quality, action, affection, place, time, posture, relation, and state. Why there are ten of them and exactly why exactly these were chosen is still not clear. The key category is substance, which he speaks about, in a dual sense in the *Categories*.

Firstly, "A substance – that which is called a substance most strictly, primarily, and most of all – is that which is neither said of a subject nor in a subject, e.g. the individual man or the individual horse" (*Cat.* 2a13-15). The substance in this first meaning is a so-called first substance (*proté úsia*) and as such is the essence of the subject itself (*hypokeimenon*, lat. *subiectum* or *substantia*). The fact that it is not said of means that it is an individual thing in its particularity,[10] which we cannot grasp using language in any way, at most we can show it as "this here"(*tode ti*). Subject is a sort of foundation, a base that can be determined.

Secondly: "The species in which the things primarily called substances are, are called *secondary substances,* as also are the genera of these species. For example, the individual man belongs in a species, man, and animal is a genus of the species; so these—both man and animal—are called secondary substances" (*Cat.* 2a15-18). In the second sense we are dealing with the second substance (*úsia deutera*) that in contrast to the first substance is said of the particular subject. This second substance is something general, namely species and genus. From the above mentioned it should be obvious what

---

10 On Aristotle's concepts of "said of/not said of" and "is/is not in" some subjects see Studtmann 2013.

Aristotle understands under the concepts "is said" or "is not said of the subject." In the first case these are specific particulars (first substances), in the second case these are the concepts expressing species or genus (the second substances).

The first and as well as the second substance Aristotle distinguishes not only according to what is indicated about the subject but also by what is in the *subject*. This type of statement matches the characteristics, which come within the remaining nine categories. What does it mean that the characteristics are *in* the subject? These features are not essential, but random, and that to exist they must be placed on some substance as their carrier. The substance itself is something durable and unchanging; the other categories represent what may be changed. Aristotle relies on the example of colour. The specific cube is white. Whiteness is thus universal, which indicates this particular cube. But whiteness is the feature only of this specific object and it can be changed if the cube's colour is changed to blue. Whiteness is therefore not a separable substance (in terms of a kind of Platonic ideas); on the other hand, it can only exist thanks to the substance that carries it.

Therefore, Aristotle distinguishes between a separable category, as in both of the mentioned senses, and inseparable categories as is substance. These categories are called inseparable because they can exist only as the certain features of substances (cannot be "separated" from the substance). Hence, they are attributes, accidents, which exist on substances only "incidentally" (*symbebékos*). Furthermore, while the substance is still the same, the individual attributes vary. For example, a specific individual, Socrates (first substance) as a person (second substance) is pale (quality), located in the Agora (place) to chat (activity) or is slandered (affection) and so on. However, if Socrates is tanned, no longer pale, the Agora may be transferred to Kalli's house and instead of chatting, he can contemplate and instead of slandering someone can admire him. Therefore accidents change, but until Socrates exists, he is still Socrates and a man. For better clarity see the displayed table of categories:

Categories	
Separable	**Inseparable:** "incidentally" (*symbebékos*)
Substance(*úsia, substantia*) First substance (*protéúsia*): subject (*hypokeimenon*) Second subject (*deteraúsia*): species (*eidos*), genus (*genos*)	**Attributes, accidents:** Quantity, quality, action, affection, place, time, posture, relation, state

4. Metaphysics and the Structure of the *Cosmos*

Already in Categories Aristotle emphasises that the subject, a specific, individual object is a substance in the truest sense of the word. It is exactly metaphysics that is devoted to the examination of basic principles, which constitute the subject. We have mentioned that he never used the term "metaphysics" instead he spoke about the "first philosophy" (*proté filosofia*), sometimes he also called it theology or wisdom (*sophia*). Already in these terms, we can see that metaphysics plays a central role and in comparison to the other areas of philosophy, it carries a certain preference. It is a science that knows "everything" because it is the highest and most abstract doctrine, which examines being as being (*on hé on*). Aristotle further describes the nature of metaphysics in the sixth book of *Metaphysics*. Each science deals with certain subjects and thus a being and its corresponding causes. The doctor, for example, deals with the human body and examines the causes of healthy and unhealthy conditions of the body; mathematics is devoted to numbers and the relationship between them and the subject of physics is a moving and variable body and the causes of its movements. Metaphysics goes further not only "beyond" physics, but also beyond other disciplines. None of the above-mentioned theories deal with being as such, but only with certain types of being, or more precisely, a certain segment of reality, while the other aspects are disregarded. For example, mathematics is interested in being, as it is countable, on the other hand medicine only as much as it can be healthy or ill. Therefore, similar to Plato's parable of line, Aristotle also notes that the scientist relates to the basic assumption that he does not problematise but accepts them. The metaphysician, however, again like Plato's dialectician goes beyond these assumptions and examines the first and most general origins (*archai*) and causes (*aitia*).

What are these causes and origins? Aristotle in several places presents a theory about the four causes of movement (cf. *Phys.* 198a14-198b5; *Met.*1013a24 ff.): the material cause (*causa materialis*), the formal cause (*causa formalis*), the effecient cause (*causa efficiens*), and finally the final cause (*causa finalis*). These causes can be discussed using the appropriate example of making a silver bowl (Heidegger, 10). To make it, we would need some material, namely silver, that represents the material cause. That is not enough, because the object must have the required form (*morfé*), respectively the shape (*eidos*) of a bowl, so this is a formal cause. Someone, however, must change the piece of silver into a bowl, so he must somehow affect it – it is done by the artisan who makes it, and this represents the efficient cause. Finally, the bowl comes into existence due to some objective or purpose to serve, such as a ceremony, and this represents the final cause. Aristotle, however, noticed a remarkable thing: efficient and final causes are already contained in the form, so they in certain sense are the formal cause. How is this possible? The purpose, for which the bowl was made, must be clear even before production starts. If the bowl should serve as a bowl for offerings, and we do not want, for example, those to fall out when it is carried, we have to adapt its shape. Finally, an artisan acting as an efficient cause must know the right shape he is giving to a piece of silver, so the form of the bowl is in his mind even before he starts to produce.

Therefore, we have two fundamental causes of *matter* (*hylé*) and *form* (*morfé*); these are the bases for the name of this – *hylomorphism*. According to Aristotle exactly this pair of principles constitute a single thing. Thus, he departs from Plato, for whom only general ideas existed truly and fully, the perceivable animate and inanimate things are only their imperfect imitations.

Every single thing is composed of matter and form. While matter is a passive principle, characterised by absence, *sterésis* (lat. *privatio*), this means it is undetermined, but it is also has the ability to accept some determination. In contrast, the form is an active principle, which pushes determination into matter. It is literally a form of *to ti en einai*, "what was to be" or essence. Form represents *eidos*, which makes a thing what it is. In other words, matter has no determination, but is able to accept it, and what exactly determines matter is form.[11] Moreover, matter is responsible for ensuring that the thing is individual and that we can meet the multiplicity and diversity of things. The form represents what the things have in common, it does not appear and disappear, and thanks to it, we can recognise things. In this respect, it is similar to Plato's concept of ideas. For example, Socrates is an individual, but what determines him is the *eidos* or form of a "man." Socrates has this essential feature in common with all people, but he also differs from them, for he has a specific height, facial features, and so on and these specifics and differences as well individuality correspond to substance. Socrates as an individual may disappear but not the human form.

According to Aristotle, matter matches the *option*, respectively the *potency* (*dynamis*) and shape matches *actuality*, respectively *act* (*energeia*). The concepts of

---

[11] In this sense, we can easily identify the principle substance with matter. The substance here is an utmost imaginary principle to which we can meet only in specified by shape.

possibility and reality allow the reasoning of movement and change. The potency represents what a thing can be, but is not yet. For example, a person who is uneducated, later can become educated, his possibility is "to be educated." In contrast, actuality represents the current state of an object. *Change is therefore the transition from potency to actuality.* The actuality, however, is not equal to the potency, but in some important respects, it prevails. In the first case, it is the priority of time in the sense of affecting cause. Some potency is brought into actuality by other object that is already in this state of actuality. For example, something currently cold may only be heated by something that is currently hot. Aristotle often mentions the phrase "man begets man" (Met. 1033b30), as proof of the priority of form and actuality. A child is not a mature, adult man only as an option, but he "inherited" that option from his adult parents who "caused" him. But the actuality prevails also in terms of the purpose. For example, plants and animals do not change randomly, but obey their internal options that are their purpose. Rose seeds do not exist to be the seeds, but to become the rose. If the rose grows from it, it updates its options, in which its existence is fully and perfectly realised. The form of the rose is hence already present in the seed. Aristotle calls this movement towards an internally given possibility as the purpose as *entelecheia*, it is a movement that "holds purpose in itself" (cf. Graeser, 313).

The emphasis on form, respectively *eidos* as reality in terms of affecting and purpose causes points out that Aristotle's understanding of the universe is largely "biological" or "functionally organic." Every living organism is a combination of soul, which is a form, and body that is matter. Therefore, according to Aristotle soul and body do not exist separately: "The body and soul are one, as is wax and its shape. The soul is the first actuality of the body, without which the body would not be a body. It gives the ability of the body to have its life processes"(Ricken, 117). Therefore, the spirit in both animals and humans and the target acting cause. *Eidos* "man" is not only the "form" of a thing that looks like man, but it is recorder in it that this creature can move, it can move other things (acting cause), also where this thing is heading to and what can or wants to achieve (the target cause).

Thus, in summary we can say that thanks to matter and form, potency and actuality the *cosmos* is an organised unit, which is characterised by movement and changeability arranged thanks to the persistence of and eternal forms: "Without matter as a versatile potency there would not be change and motion in the world. Always shapeless as without a certain form, the world would be nothing but chaos if it does not arise" (Martinka, 376).

We have mentioned that Aristotle sometimes calls the first philosophy wisdom or theology, because he is heading towards recognition of the highest causes. Therefore, metaphysics is not limited only to hylomorphic interpretation of the causes of specific beings, but also to an understanding of God. Aristotle labels God as the *first, motionless mover*, which is the first and the last cause of all that exists. Motionless mover is specific because it is *pure act*, and thus differs from other beings that are merged from matter and form, potency and actuality. Therefore it does not contain any potency and of course no matter. Since matter and form are conditions of movement, change, and creation and termination, the motionless mover as pure actuality is eternal, without any change and still the same, he thinks himself, and is perfect and blessed.

According to Aristotle, God must necessarily exist. In order to clarify his reasoning, we must briefly turn our attention for some moments to Aristotle's ideas of physics and the *cosmos*. His vision is geocentric; in its centre is the Earth that is surrounded by a revolving Moon, the Sun, planets, and stars. Therefore, we can talk about three levels: firstly, the sub-lunar sphere where we live. This area is characterised by the four elements (fire, water, earth, air), and here movement takes the form not only of local movement from place to place, but also changes in the form of creation and destruction. Above this area is a sphere of planets, which are in constant local movement, which do not happen in a perfect circle. This movement, however, lasts forever, so the Sun,

Moon and planets are characterised by immortality. The highest area is the sphere of planets, which perpetually move in perfect circles. According to Aristotle, the perfect circular motion of the stars is the cause of the movements in the lower levels, which are manifested in our sub-lunar sphere, for example, by the changing seasons and so on.

The core of Aristotle's argument in favour of the existence of the motionless mover lies in the fact that movement is possible because actuality as well as potency are present in things. However the result is that what exists, must not necessarily exist. If the planets are in motion, they must have the potency for motion in themselves. However, if they have the potency, they also cannot provide the eternal movement from themselves. Nevertheless, the planets are in eternal, continuous movement and therefore something must keep them moving. Therefore, there must be a God who is pure reality without potency, and thus this guarantees the circular motion of the planets.

According to Aristotle, the world is eternal and uncreated, and therefore there is the question of in what sense God is the cause of motion. God is not the mover in the meaning of the Creator, but is the highest good, which moves all *in the way of the beloved*, as "the object of love" (*Met*.1072b3). As the highest and perfect good is an object of desire. According to Aristotle, everything that exists, wants to become similar to God as much as possible. Therefore, in their perfect circular and perpetual motion the planets are approaching God. Similarly, all living things desire God. A living creature is naturally mortal, but achieves immortality by maintaining its life and especially its immortal genus in the cycle of life and death.

Aristotle's idea of reality and the universe is thus a hierarchical pattern based on expediency. Highest in the hierarchy stands the motionless mover as the first and last cause of everything, followed by a region of celestial bodies and our earthly sub-lunar sphere where everything animate and inanimate is determined to achieve their own perfection that fulfils the purpose set out in its *eidos*.

5. Ethics

Ethics deal with an area of human experience, and therefore it occupies a special place among the sciences. This is explained in the sixth book of *Nicomachean Ethics* (1139b15-1140b9), where Aristotle distinguishes between theoretical knowledge (*epistémé*), the art of creating things (*techné*), and practical wisdom (*fronésis*), which is crucial to ethics. It is possible to criticise this distinction, but it is sufficient for the understanding of the nature of experience. Knowledge is theoretical and its necessary subject is a being, such a being that cannot be otherwise. On the contrary, art as well as practical sanity deal with the accidental, contingent being, which is in one way, but it may be also otherwise. An example of theoretical knowledge is mathematics that deals with the natural relationships between numbers and geometric figures. For example, it is always true that the sum of the interior angles of a triangle is 180°; it will never be more or less. A contingent being is for example a sick person who cannot be healthy. Knowledge thus proceeds to the truths regarding the necessary being. This way it differs from art and understanding. The object of art is a creative activity that has an acting cause of its creator, but a purpose in the created subject. The subject of creative activity is thus, as opposed to theoretical knowledge, a contingent, random thing that indeed exists, but need not to exist. The subject of practical rationality is moral practice and action (*praxis*), where one tries to achieve the highest practicable good. Given that practice is variable and that we are acting always from a certain single position, we are dealing with random beings. Our practical rationality, therefore, is heading to the true judgment about the correct action for a given situation.

Why is it necessary to make a distinction between theoretical leadership and ethics as a practical science? Theoretical science can proceed deductively; with the help of formal rules that may come from certain general arguments concerning the unchanging, necessary being, to other necessarily true statements. Given that the sum of the two interior angles of a triangle is 90°, we can deduce that the triangle is right-angled because the third angle is necessarily a right angle. However, this approach in practice is not very helpful. Since these proceedings are always set in a particular, always-unique situation, the answer to the question how we should act appropriately, cannot be deduced from general principles. Ethics as a science of procedure does not provide us with rules that we can always clearly apply everywhere. It is at best probabilistic, it can tell us only what is approximately right.

According to Aristotle, neither moral conduct nor proper recognition is innate. However, we are born with skills to gain these abilities during our lives. This shows that we must gradually learn to recognise for a given situation which action is right, in a way that we simply try to act properly and *become used to it*. In other words, we can become moral only if we practise morality, we have certain experiences.[12] From this is derived the concept of ethics. The etymological origin of the term is *ethos* (EN 1103a15-20). *Ethos* means "habit" in a dual sense: firstly, it is a convention, customs traditionalised in a community; secondly, the habit of a person to act in a certain way. A morally good person is so accustomed to acting properly that it happens as if it were his "second nature." Aristotle is thus a critic of the "Socratic" notion according to which it is enough to know what is good to act correctly. His position is a bit more complex. While we

---

12 Therefore, in the *Nicomachean Ethics*, Aristotle notes that practical philosophy (ethics and politics) are not intended for young people, but only for mature, adult people who already have certain experience of practical actions.

know what and how to act in a certain situation, but if we are not sufficiently accustomed to the correct procedure, we can act in a different way.

Aristotle's idea of purpose that pervades the entire *cosmos* also appears in his practical philosophy. The aim of life is *eudaimonia*, which is usually translated as "bliss," "happiness," or "success" (Synek, 20-21). Everything that exists tries to fulfil some purpose during its existence. Aristotle distinguishes three types of purpose, which we can follow by our activities. The first type is purpose that we wish not for directly, but for something else. For example, to work, this means exertion, trouble, that we usually do not want just because of the work, but because we need to earn a living. The second type is the purpose that we want because of itself and of something else. Such a purpose is, for example, a reputation that we want not only to acquire good friends, but also for its own sake. Finally, the third type of purpose is that which we want only because of the purpose itself. Bliss is such a purpose. Bliss is an independent purpose, because we do not want it for any other reason. Therefore, the question why (for what) we wish to be blessed makes no sense to us; we simply want to be blessed. According to Aristotle everything we do in our lives, we do to achieve *eudaemonia*. Therefore, for us it is the highest good, and all other goals are subordinate to it.

The concept of *eudaemonia* is not entirely clear, but includes two moments. First, we can be blessed only if we have virtue (*arete*): "bliss (*eudaemonia*) is a kind of activity of the soul in terms of perfect virtue (*aretén*)" (EN 1102a5). We mentioned that the soul is the shape of our body, and that *eidos* is not only an affecting but also a purpose cause. Therefore, we can be blessed only if our soul is in its best (*aristos*) state. According to Aristotle, there are several components to our soul: it has a growth and nutritious component, then sentient, lust (*epithymétikon*), and reason (*logos*). Our soul is in the best condition when these components are reasonably active, if they fulfil their purpose. In terms of ethics, the most important components of the soul are lust and reason (EN 1101a25-1103a5). Lust is an irrational component, which heads towards what appears to be good for it. Although it is separated from reason, but is able to obey reason. Reason is the highest component of the soul, which on the one hand proceeds to knowledge, and on the other hand, allows us to distinguish in practice what does not only seem right and good, but also what is really right and good. Aristotle in his teaching presents a similar experience of mental conflict as Plato did in the Republic (EN 1102b14-18). Since the mind is the highest component of the human soul, just by using it we can achieve happiness as our purpose in life, which means that the component of lust should be subject to reason and allow reason to cultivate it. Otherwise, the soul is in inner disharmony and fails in its purpose. According to these components Aristotle divides up the virtues of ethic (*Ethics*), which relate the component of lust and *dianoethic* (intellectual) as relating to the component of reason (*EN* 1103a1-10).

Secondly, virtue itself is not enough for bliss, because even the most virtuous person may be exposed to the negative effects of chance (*tyché*), of unfortunate events over which he has no control. Aristotle mentioned the Trojan king Priam as an example (*EN* 1101a8). The Aristotelian requirements for bliss are maximalist. We can speak about a blissful life only if it was so from birth to death and if it was not affected by any adverse circumstances. Aristotle with his maximal demands is a realist and warns that man is an imperfect being living in an imperfect world. The ideal of bliss can be only approached. Therefore, virtue is a necessary condition for happiness, but certainly not a sufficient condition. In other words, it is possible that a virtuous man exists that due to the actions of chance is not quite blissful; but it is impossible that someone, who is not virtuous is blessed. However, it is not irrelevant whether a virtuous or non-virtuous person faces the negative events of life. While the first of them bears these events with dignity, the other one succumbs to them and suffers.

We have mentioned that the component lust is indeed unreasonable, but is able to listen to reason. While reason cultivates it, the soul gains ethical virtues. We acquire these virtues through habit, by repeated activities. It is important to note that Aristotle's ethics also have an emotional dimension. The component lust is characterised by the ability to desire something. As far as it lacks a subject it desires, it falls, because it does not fulfil its purpose. However, it reaches its goal, when it does not want only an apparent good, but a real good, that is shown by reason.

According to Aristotle an ethical virtue is always a sort of midpoint (*meson*) with respect to two opposite extremes, one of which is a surplus and the second a need. For example, generosity is the ability that forms the midpoint between frugality on one side and profligacy on the other. A generous person gives adequately to those who deserve it and when they need it. In contrary, a frugal one does not give enough, that is, not as much as is appropriate and the profligate one gives away too much, regardless of the adequacy of the situation and whether the recipient deserves or needs it. Another example is courage, which is the midpoint between cowardice on one side and fearlessness on the other. A brave person can recognise the real extent of the danger he faces. In contrast, the coward sees a looming threat larger than it really is and a daredevil[13] flouts it. It is understandable that when an ethic virtue is the midpoint in one sense, in the other sense it is a modification of human mental possibilities it stands as the highest value above the extremes. Generosity and boldness are only examples of

---

13 Neither Aristotle nor we currently have adequate term for this extreme. Cf. *EN* 1107b1-5.

ethic virtue and we should add that Aristotle does not display the whole list. The most important ethic virtue is justice, which relates to the relationships with other people and it can cause other virtues to vary because it includes them (EN 1130a1-15). According to Plato, justice is hence an ethic virtue that a person has only if he disposes of the others.

The cultivation of the component lust is also reflected in the attitude towards life. A virtuous man is blissful, unless adverse external circumstances hinder him. However, that does not mean that every person who acts rightly is at the same time happy because of his actions. The only one who is happy is the one who is virtuous and who wants to so act. There are occasions when many people apparently act properly, but they are not blissful, and often they are forced to act by outer pressure, otherwise they would not want to act appropriately. Thus, we can distinguish different types of people based on how they act and how happy they are due to their behaviour. The *virtuous* act properly, they want to do so and take joy from it. The *moderate* are on lower level. Although they want to act badly, they moderate themselves and act properly, but they are not happy. *Immoderate* people are characterised by a weak will and therefore after some reluctance they choose the bad action. At the lowest level are the non-virtuous who act badly without hesitation. Their life is the farthest from bliss because their souls live in conflict and disharmony.

In the sixth book of *Nicomachean Ethics*, after analysing the ethic virtues Aristotle proceeds to a description of the rational component whose task is to cultivate lust. The *virtues* can be divided according to the subject to which they are related. Our mind can focus on either the essential being or the random being. Unless we focus on the essential being, we indulge in a theoretical, philosophical life (*bios theoretikos*) and can acquire the virtue of knowledge (*episteme*), (theoretical) wisdom (*sofia*) and (intuitive) understanding (*nús*). Understanding is related to the understanding of the fundamental and highest principles, while knowledge is the true understanding of the eternal being that results from these principles. According to Aristotle, the highest dianoetic virtue is wisdom, which includes knowledge and understanding (EN 1141a17-21). We should not forget that wisdom is one of the first terms of philosophy.

While the mind focuses on the random being, it can acquire skill (*techné*) by creating objects of art. For ethics and Practical life, reasonableness is the most important, respectively practical wisdom (*fronésis*). It is important not only in private life, but also and perhaps especially in public life (*bios politikos*). According to Aristotle through *fronésis*, we are able to recognise what is beneficial for a particular situation with respect to our lives as a whole, as well as for other members of the community and the city, "rationality is an unmistakable (mental) state of reasonable acts in things that are good and bad for people"(EN 1141b5). Since in action we deal with variable and contingent events, reasonability is not the same as knowledge concerning the eternal and unchanging. Therefore, prior experience of individual cases is required so we may act properly.

An interesting and still contentious issue of Aristotle's practical philosophy is the issue of whether theoretical or political life is better. We have mentioned that Aristotle's universe is arranged so that everything within it tries to approach, to conform to a motionless mover as the first and final cause of everything. Man not only achieves this by ensuring his survival and the survival of his family, but especially that he fulfils his own internal options that are written in his soul. In other words, when he tries to live well, blissfully, and virtuously. As the highest component of the soul is the mind, we approach the motionless mover by recognising it as the first cause, and that we grasp eternal and unchanging being, thus conducting the reasonable component utmost. Therefore, according to Aristotle, we can be blissful if we do not live a philosophical way of life.

It would be a mistake to believe that *fronésis* is therefore unnecessary for a blissful life. Man is an entity by his very nature, designed for life in the political community:

"Hence it is evident that the city is a creation of nature, and that man is by nature a political animal. And he who by nature and not by mere accident is without a city, is either a bad man or above humanity" (*Pol.* 1253a1 –4). Life in the city is a purpose of human life and so "he who is unable to live in a society ... must be either a beast or a god" (*Pol.* 1253a28-29). Since life in a community with others is our purpose as well as our theoretical life, to achieve bliss it is not enough to use solely reason for the purpose of knowledge of the essential being and the highest causes. Our lives can be best fulfilled in the community, if we are morally virtuous, so if we adequately use common sense based on the unique situations of moral practice.

List of Abbreviations

Arist.	–	Aristotle
Cat.	–	Categories
Met.	–	Metaphysics
EN	–	Nicomachean Ethics
Pol.	–	Politics

Plat.	–	Plato
Crat.	–	Kratylos
Ep.	–	Letters
Euthyphr.	–	Eutyphron
Meno	–	Meno
Phaed.	–	Phaedo
Phaedr.	–	Phaedros
Resp.	–	Republic
Tim.	–	Timaeus

DL = Diogenes Laertios: *Lives of Eminent Philosophers*

Bibliography

Aubenque, Pierre: *Problém bytí u Aristotela*. Praha: Oikoymenh 2014.
Aubenque, Pierre: *Rozumnost podle Aristotela*. Praha: Oikoymenh 2003.
Barnes, Jonathan (ed.): *The Complete Works of Aristotle. Volume I.* Princeton 1984.
Barnes, Jonathan (ed.): *The Complete Works of Aristotle. Volume II.* Princeton 1984.
Cooper, John M. – Hutchinson, D. S. (eds.) *Plato. Complete Works.* Indianapolis: Hacket 1997.
Diogenes Laertius: *Lives of Eminent Philosophers. Volume I. Books 1-5.* Cambridge, Mass.: Harvard University Press 1972.
Gadamer, Hans-Georg: *Idea Dobra mezi Platónema Aristotelem.* Praha: Oikoymenh 2010.
Graeser, A.: *Řecká filosofie klasického období.* Praha: Oikoymenh 2000.
Heidegger, M.: Otázka techniky. In: *Věda, technika a zamyšlení.* Praha: Oikoymenh 2004.
Martinka, Jaroslav: Dominanty antickej filozofie. In: Scruton, R.: *Krátke dejiny novovekej filozofie. Od Descarta po Wittgensteina.* Bratislava: Archa 1991.
Kratochvíl, Zdeněk: *Filosofie medzi mýtem a vědou. OdHoméra po Descartesa.* Praha: Academia 2010.

Nussbaum, M.: *The Fragility of Goodness. Luck and Ethics in Greek Tragedy and Philosophy*. Cambridge: Cambridge University Press 2001.

Patočka, Jan: *Platónova péče o duši a spravedlivý stát*. Praha: Oikoymenh 2012.

Peterman, John: *On Plato*. Wadsworth 2002.

Porubjak, Matúš: Priateľstvo ako cnosť súkromná i verejná. In: *Ostium*, roč. 4, č. 1, 2008a.

Porubjak, Matúš: Problém *anamnésis* a Platónov dialóg *Menón*. In: *Filozofia*, roč. 63, č. 1, 2008b.

Porubjak, Matúš – Vydra, Anton: Zoznam skratiek vybraných antických autorov a ich diel. In: *Ostium*, roč. 4, č. 3, 2008.

Ricken, Friedo: *Antická filosofie*. Olomouc: Nakladatelství Olomouc 1999.

Shields, Christopher: Aristotle. In: *The Stanford Encyclopedia of Philosophy* (Spring 2014 Edition), Edward N. Zalta (ed.), URL = <http://plato.stanford.edu/archives/spr2014/entries/aristotle/>.

Studtmann, Paul: Aristotle's Categories. In: *The Stanford Encyclopedia of Philosophy* (Summer 2014 Edition), Edward N. Zalta (ed.), URL = <http://plato.stanford.edu/archives/sum2014/entries/aristotle-categories/>.

Synek, Stanislav: *Lidská přirozenost jako úkol člověka. Filosofická interpretace Etiky Nikomachovy*. Praha: Togga 2011.

Thein, Karel: Nepřesná analogie. Spravodlivá obec, části duše a člověk v Platónově Ústavě. In: *Myšlení v nás. Tři platónske studie*. Praha: Filosofia 2010, 245-313.

Voegelin, Eric: *The New Science of Politics: An Introduction*. In: Henningsen, Manfred (ed.): *The Collected Works of Eric Voegelin. Volume 5. Modernity without Restraint*. Columbia: University of Missouri 2000, 75-241.

Vydra, Anton: *Akademické písanie. Ako vzniká filozofický text*. Trnava: FF TU 2010.

Wyller, Egil A.: *Pozdní Platón. Tübingenské přednášky 1965*. Praha: Petr Rezek 1996.

Michal Zvarík works as a lecturer at the Department of Philosophy at Faculty of Philosophy and Arts, Trnava University. His research interests include ancient Greek philosophy, Hannah Arendt and phenomenology, mostly in relation to phenomena of a political space. In present he is providing research on intellectual virtues in Aristotle, especially on the problem of phronesis. In 2011 he published Predsudok vo fenomenológii každodennosti: *Štruktúra predsudku u Edmunda Husserla, Alfreda Schütza a Martina Heideggera* and in 2013 co-translated Home & Beyond: *Generative Phenomenology after Husserl*, by Anthony Steinbock into Slovak.

Európska únia
Európsky sociálny fond

Európska únia

Operačný program
VZDELÁVANIE

VÝSKUMNÁ AGENTÚRA

www.ingramcontent.com/pod-product-compliance
Ingram Content Group UK Ltd.
Pitfield, Milton Keynes, MK11 3LW, UK
UKHW041920140426
5217IPUK00014B/243